WRITERS' BRITAIN

ENGLISH COUNTRY HOUSES

In the same series

British Dramatists Graham Greene
The English Poets Lord David Cecil
Life Among the English Rose Macaulay

ENGLISH COUNTRY HOUSES

VITA SACKVILLE-WEST

with
8 plates in colour
and
16 illustrations in
black & white

PRION

This edition published in Great Britain by Prion Books Ltd.,
32-34 Gordon House Road,
London, NW5 1LP

First published in 1941 by Collins

A catalogue record of this book can be obtained
from the British Library

ISBN 1-85375-230-4

Jacket by Andrea Purdie based on the original design
Typeset by York House Typographic Ltd, London
Colour origination by MRM Graphics, Singapore
Printed & bound in Singapore

I

THERE IS NOTHING QUITE LIKE THE ENGLISH COUNTRY house anywhere else in the world. France has her châteaux, Italy her historic villas, Spain her gardens like the Generalife hooked on to the hillside, Germany her robber castles, but the exact equivalent of what we mean by the English country house is not to be found elsewhere.

It may be large, it may be small; it may be palatial, it may be manorial; it may be of stone, brick, stucco, or even of beams and plaster; it may be the seat of the aristocracy or the home of the gentry – whatever it is, it possesses one outstanding characteristic: it is the English country house.

You may observe that I do not put a hyphen between the two words. I write 'country house,' not 'country-house.' This is deliberate. It is because I want to emphasise that the house is essentially part of the country, not only *in* the country, but part of it, a natural growth. Irrespective of grandeur or modesty, it should agree with its landscape and suggest the life of its inhabitants past or present; should never overwhelm its surroundings. The peculiar genius of the English country house lies in its knack of fitting in.

Wotton in Surrey, seat of diarist John Evelyn, 1862.

II

THE ENGLISH ARE A RURAL-MINDED PEOPLE ON THE whole, which perhaps explains why our rural domestic architecture is so much better than our urban. Our cities, generally speaking, are deplorable. There is a lack of design which must make the French smile. When the French hint delicately at this we are apt to murmur 'Bath,' and then come to a full stop. Challenged further, we produce Oxford and Cambridge; and then fall back on certain cathedral towns: York, Durham, Salisbury, Canterbury. Challenged again, we fall back on our third line of defence: our small country towns, say Chippenham, or Abingdon, Burford, Painswick, Devizes, Lewes. Challenged once more, we fall back on the fourth line where we find ourselves in an even stronger position. We have not been able to put up much defence for our cities, but once we are reduced to fighting on our villages we have a number of outposts. Their names are too many to record. We all have our favourites which come to the mind with a vision of moors or a memory of running water; hidden amongst trees or gazing across the sea; grey stone villages, pink brick villages; villages of the soft south country or the north, they belong to the soil in the same sense as the country house belongs to the soil and indeed are frequently and happily associated with it. The cottage, the farm, and the manor are the same in spirit.

III

IF THIS PREMISE BE ACCEPTED, IT MUST FOLLOW THAT some types of our country houses satisfy our demands better than others. And, since it would be idle to write so brief and unprofessional a monograph as this from any but the most personal point of view, prejudiced possibly but certainly offered with conviction, I must insist from the start that some of our major country houses (more properly to be called 'seats') seem to me to be excrescences which should never have defaced the countryside. These are the exceptions. It is not a question of size. Some of our major and most famous houses accord with their surroundings as quietly as their little cousins. Others most emphatically do not. The reason for this is that they were too often built all of a piece, to gratify the ostentation of some rich man in an age when display meant more than beauty; they were not allowed to grow with the oaks and elms and beeches; they were not true country houses at all, but a deliberate attempt to reproduce in the country the wealth and fame which their owner enjoyed in town. They were his country residence rather than his home. They were false to the real tradition. They do not represent England at all, and, although they must be mentioned and even illustrated in the following pages, it must be understood that the sympathies of the author of this monograph are not with them, but follow a more modest range. Thus, although Chatsworth, Stowe, Blenheim, Welbeck, Bowood, Castle Howard, Wentworth Woodhouse, to instance only a few, have their splendours, they cannot be said to melt into England or to share the simple graciousness of her woods and fields. They are as much out of place here in England as Versailles or Vaux-le-Vicomte are in place in France. They do not represent the peculiar English genius for domestic architecture. They are usually the work of a single eminent architect, not of the anonymous builders who in successive centuries added a piece here, an ornamentation there, as the needs and taste and resources of the owners changed. They may have the advantage of architectural unity; from the other point of view, more sentimental perhaps, less romantic, they lack the advantage of a natural development. And it must be added that the unity is frequently of a style not to be admired.

IV

IT WAS DIFFICULT TO DECIDE HOW TO ARRANGE A SHORT monograph like this. Obviously it was impossible to mention or to illustrate more than a very small number of the houses that ought to be mentioned and illustrated. The question was a double one: first, which to select; and second, the most convenient order in which to discuss them. One might do it in several ways: by date, by county, by size and fame, by material (brick, stone, black and white). All things considered, it seemed best to do it by date. That meant beginning with the castles. But then, immediately, everything began to overlap. Castles cropped up in centuries where they had no business at all, and, although the need for fortification had ceased to exist, the liking for it romantically persisted. What, for instance, were Maxstoke and Broughton doing in the fourteenth century? or little Nunney, later still? or Hurstmonceux raising its lovely machicolated towers in the reign of Henry VI? Clearly, the English dwelling refused to be pigeon-holed. Then there were the additions, separated sometimes by several hundred years. Broughton jumped from 1300 to 1590; Knole from King John to King James; Compton Wynyates grew in a leisurely way between 1450 and 1520, then wandered, still growing, through the Eighteenth century, and came finally to rest somewhere in the middle of the nineteenth. If my English houses were to be treated chronologically it became manifest that the classification must in many cases be very elastic indeed. This realisation, inconvenient though it might be, did however confirm the theory that the charm and genius of our domestic architecture lay in its gradual and continuous development. It was possible also to work out that development on the guiding lines of our internal history, through periods of tumult into periods of prosperity and peace at home; the control of the Crown, the power of the barons, the quiet security of the squire, the rise of the middle class, the flowering of the great servants of the State, the insolence of the later aristocracy – all were represented in the homes they created for themselves in their increasingly peaceful land. For it must be remembered that the English house owes much to the relative peace which this island has enjoyed internally since the Norman Conquest. The Conquest itself was less of a convulsion than (eventually) a force of unification. The wars of England – the Crusades, the Hundred Years' War – took her kings abroad; the wars of Edward I, Edward II and Edward III took them to

Wales and Scotland; the wars with Spain and France were not fought on English soil. The Wars of the Roses were not of the kind that devastate a country, and indeed it remains for Cromwell to claim the dishonour of doing greater damage in England by an Englishman than any which had gone before or has followed since. Fortunate in her domestic history, it seems likely that England (who in accordance with her tradition once again escaped invasion in the recent war) will witness the gradual destruction of her lovely inheritance by economic rather than violent means.

Compton Wynyates, Warwickshire.

V

HAVING DECIDED, THEN, TO TREAT MY SUBJECT chronologically so far as was possible, without tying myself down to any unbreakable rule, I turned to the castles, and here found that my task was simplified by the fact that no uninhabited castle could possibly be considered as a country house. Ruins were not for me. Without regret I discarded those imposing but purely defensive wrecks which once guarded our coasts, our cities, the Welsh marches and Scottish border, but I still thought ruefully of those which might be called the more intimate castles, not really castles in the true sense of the term, since they were never intended to withstand an attacking force, but which carried on the tradition of feudalism long after the necessity for defence had disappeared. Some of them, indeed, were no more than manor-houses pretending to be fortified; others, again, were obviously inspired by the *châteaux-forts* which had taken the fancy of the builder during his service in the French wars. They were visions of chivalry, not

Alnwick Castle, Northumberland.

strongholds. There was Stokesay in Salop, where Sir Lawrence of Ludlow went to the quite unnecessary trouble of obtaining the royal licence to crenellate; Scotney in Sussex, which still dreams amongst its flaming azaleas above its dark-green moat; Nunney in Somerset, a tiny copy of the Paris Bastille; Bodiam in Sussex (which certainly might have aspired to defend its valley against a French invader), remaining uncompleted, with rounded towers rising out of a floor of water-lilies. All these for one reason or another could find no place in my book: either they were deserted or else they were ruined. But there were plenty of others, and I found no difficulty in believing the statement of one authority that at one time no less than fifteen hundred castles stood on English soil.

I had to make my choice amongst castles that remained and could still be counted as country houses. The huge ducal pair, Arundel and Alnwick, one in the far south, the other in the far north, immediately came to mind. They were comparable in many respects: both dominated the country from their hillsides; both sprawled above a little river, the Arun or the Aln; both took their history back to Norman times; both echoed with the names that resound through Shakespeare – Howard and Percy, Norfolk and Northumberland. So far so good. But in another respect they were also comparable, and this spoilt them both. Tremendous piles though they are, seen from a distance, a closer view showed that the Norman keep of Arundel, the Norman arches of Alnwick, had been buried inside the rebuilding and restoration of a century which loved Gothic for its own spiky sake, battlements for their associations, and towers for the proclamation of lordships. Arundel and Alnwick, in a word, were large and largely fakes.

There was a castle, however, away in another corner of England completing an irregular triangle with the other two; a castle as richly looped to English history, a castle which in no sense could be called a fake. Sullen, secretive, it looked and still looks across the bright green water-meadows towards the Severn where sea-gulls circle and the wild geese fly. Nothing but its colour and its beauty could save it from being wholly tragic and sinister. Its history is tragic enough, for it records the murder of an English king. Edward II died there in 1327 after five months of imprisonment, with the knowledge and connivance of his host. Indignities had been heaped upon him throughout the summer months from April to September; his jailers placed putrid carcases in his prison and shaved him with ditch-water and crowned him with hay to make a mock of him before his dreadful end. Dark tales; but Berkeley Castle is not dark. Not even the great yews on the terrace, cut into the shapes of elephants carrying howdahs on their backs, can sadden its beauty. It is rose-red and grey, red sandstone and grey stone, the colour of old brocade; the colour of pot-pourri; then there is a sudden buttress of yellow stone, and then a dark purple lump of masonry; red valerian juts out from the cracks. Berkeley has its own peculiarities of colouring. Its own Hunt-pack assembles under its walls, the coats of the hunt servants not pink as customary in English hunting scenes, but canary-yellow. Berkeley has a swagger of its own.

The same proud family has held it for eight hundred years. It must be the oldest inhabited castle in England, built originally to defend the Severn valley against the Welsh. The water-meadows can still be flooded at will. It is fitting to think that the first English translation of the Bible was made here (if we may accept the authority of Caxton, our first English printer) by John Trevisa, the local vicar and private chaplain to Thomas, Lord Berkeley, when the castle was already two hundred years old. It is said that the first chapter of Genesis was painted in black letter on the chapel cloister wall. It is very English, all that, and very suitable.

After the massive secrecy of Berkeley one turns to the mirrored magic of Leeds and Broughton, floating swan-like above their moats. Leeds, fortunately for itself, is nowhere near the industrial town of that name, but lies in a hollow of Kent between Maidstone and Canterbury. Its moat is no regular geometrical moat, but a saucer of a lake spreading flat at the bottom of its bowl of green slopes. Black swans pass gravely and gracefully under the arches of the castle, making the pale grey of the walls seem even paler. The very fact that the water

Berkeley Castle, Gloucestershire.

passes under arches turns Leeds Castle into a Kentish Venice. By moonlight the solid walls have no substance; they drift, they seem scarcely moored. Broughton does not now rise quite so abruptly as Leeds out of the water. At Broughton there are lawns which interrupt the reflection, but in an unexpected way these level English lawns almost take the place of water; it is merely that they are opaque instead of translucent; they are green as water though less quivering, less sensitive to clouds or sunlight.

England is green throughout; her seas, her woods, her fields all island-green. Green, quiet England. Old, quiet England, disliking war, never having known war at home in the sense that European countries knew war. No devastation, no wrecking of villages and the homes of man, whether castle or cottage. There might be incidents as at Berkeley, where a breach was deliberately cut in the walls after Cromwell's troops had stormed the castle, a breach which exists to this day, never to be repaired, on the understanding that the castle must be handed back to the Crown if ever the gap should be mended. Such is the continuity of English history. We suffer (or enjoy) to-day the arrangements made for us several hundred years ago, a little filament of tradition running through the centuries. As a result of a siege in 1645 the eighteenth Lord Berkeley was forbidden to mend his house; to-day, nothing to do with the ordinary building restrictions, his lineal descendant may not build up his house either. A curious obligation to impose on a man in the twentieth century, to render his castle undefendable!

The continuity is indeed impressive. Lumley, its great keep blackened now by the grime of the Durham collieries, is still owned by the family which has lived on the same ground for a thousand years and which built the castle. It is true than Vanbrugh laid his hands upon the windows, but the inner courtyard still displays the quarterings of the Lumleys from William the Conqueror to Queen Elizabeth and the effigies of the Lumley Warriors lie carved in stone along the wall of the chapel.

Berkeley, Leeds, Broughton, Lumley . . . Then one thinks of other castles: Warwick, hanging over the Avon in so dangerous a way that it seems just about to pitch down into the waters and be swept away by Shakespeare's river for ever; St. Donat's, in rocky Glamorgan, compact of square towers inside the rounded outer walls; Sizergh, in Westmorland, held by the Stricklands for over six hundred years; and that strange island fortress, St. Michael's Mount, off the coast of Cornwall, rising on its rock sheer out of the sea as though it were about to be blown into flame by the torches of its red-hot pokers, staring from the embrasures of its window-seats straight across the Atlantic with nothing but ocean between itself and America from whom our help ultimately came.

All these are true castles, and I have omitted many – Naworth, Raby, Allington, Chilham's round Norman tower, and even royal Windsor – but what is one to say about such places as Maxstoke and Hurstmonceux? Are they to be regarded as castles or as country homes? Is Maxstoke to be considered as a castle, which, although it calls itself Maxstoke Castle, is no more a defensive castle than any other manor-house putting itself into a position of historically unnecessary defence? What is one to say about Hurstmonceux, unreal as theatrical scenery and even more romantic? These castles, which are not fortress castles built for military purposes, puzzle one until one realises that the castle tradition went on for years after the need for defensive castles had ceased. The habits of life were altering; the home was becoming more of a home and less of a stronghold; the relative peace and comfort of Tudor times were replacing the violence of earlier days, and the result was two-fold. The picturesque elements of the castle were retained – the moat, the gatehouse, the battlements, the drawbridge – but either they were incorporated amongst buildings better adapted to the new requirements, or else they were architecturally reproduced as 'features'.

Ightham Mote, though it cannot claim a long tenure of the same ownership and is scarcely to be termed a castle, may stand as representative of the modifications imposed upon fifteenth-century buildings. It is rightly described as 'a most engaging agglomeration of different styles (where) every age has had its say, every owner has set his mark.' It is a lost little place, with its grey stone gatehouse, brown tile roofs, patches of beam and plaster, Gothic doorways and mullioned windows.

Very much the same may be said of Maxstoke, in Warwickshire, which, although more of a castle than Ightham and lacking Ightham's varied agglomeration, yet has the seventeenth-century dwelling-house tacked on to the Plantagenet buildings. Then there is Hever in Kent, which has met with so unusual a fate that it deserves to be recorded. This grey little castle, once the home of Anne Boleyn, very square and neat within itself, came into the hands of William Waldorf Astor (later Viscount Astor), who wished to entertain week-end parties of twenty-five guests. It was clearly impossible to add a wing to a building limited by the confines of its own moat. Backed by the Astor millions, however, the new owner proceeded to build a replica of a complete Tudor village, cottages which although from the outside apparently separate were linked inside by a series of winding passages, so that no guest, once indoors, could imagine himself in anything but one vast sprawling country house.

Last on my list of castles comes Hurstmonceux, which resembles Hever in the one particular that it found a wealthy owner before becoming the property of Greenwich Observatory, as it now is. But with

Ightham Mote, Kent.

Hurstmonceux the case was different; it was not a question of additions, but of rebuilding the ruined walls and halls. Only the front of the red-brick castle remained: the two great towers of the gateway, the flanking wings, rising superbly from the green fosse which had once been the moat. Lost among the oaks and bracken of Sussex, the sea not far away, there was a beauty of desolation, a nobility in ruin which supplied a fantasy that restoration, however skilful, can never recapture.

VI

MEANWHILE, MOVING AWAY FROM THE CASTLE, THE semi-castle, or even the fortified dwelling, a different type was gradually developing in England which, from its modest beginnings, was later to find its expression in the palatial homes of the Tudor nobility. The system of grander provincial English life inevitably dictated this development. The prosperous yeoman demanded something better than the labourer's cottage; the squire demanded something better than the yeoman, the lord demanded something better than the squire, and thus by logical progression the three types of Tudor domestic architecture arose. With the yeoman's abode this is perhaps not the place to deal, since it can scarcely be ranked among the country houses, but it is still to be met with in the length and breadth of the island, characteristic of its locality, unpretentious, and so English that England would be less England without it. Our lanes and villages, farmsteads and hamlets will produce them by the score. The beams and plaster of

Kent, Sussex and Cheshire, the beams and brick of Hampshire, the stone of Wiltshire and Gloucestershire, all take their place worthily beside the more ambitious aspiration of the squire or the lord of the manor.

It is difficult to assign exact dates for the style which we roughly know as Tudor. The English genius slowly evolved its own idiom in this manner, but the very slowness of its growth renders the result confusing, and it would be perfectly possible for an untrained eye to mistake, say, a seventeenth-century Cotswold manor-house for one of the same type built at least a hundred years earlier. It is possible, again, for the late fifteenth century to stray over into the sixteenth without any loss of this general family likeness; it is difficult to believe, for instance, that such a house as Ockwells, in Berkshire, was built as early as 1450. The Gothic influence is still visible in the tall, almost ecclesiastical windows, but I doubt whether any visitor, asked for a date, would hesitate to reply 'Tudor.' Similarly a mixture of dates of construction such as may be seen at the exquisite South Wraxall, in Wiltshire (1470 or even earlier, with additions belonging to both ends of the sixteenth century) compose themselves agreeably into a whole which most people would designate as 'a Tudor manor-house.' South Wraxall claims to be the first house in England where Sir Walter Raleigh smoked his pipe.

Again, at Lacock Abbey, which stands on the outskirts of one of the most picturesque of Wiltshire villages, the confusion of dates must baffle all but the best-informed. There are the old convent buildings of the thirteenth century, cloisters of the fifteenth, a whole quadrangle and an octagonal tower dating from 1554, and a Gothic archway of 1754. To complicate matters further, the Sir William Sharington who added the quadrangle and the tower also altered the windows of the thirteenth-century part and built new chimneys. The general effect, however, is held together in surprising unity by the use of the beautiful Bath stone. Without therefore attempting any pedantic exactitude we may conveniently consider the rise of the manor-house from about 1500 to about 1650. A very brief glance at English social history will reveal the reason for the prevalence of the manor-house, and also the reason why it may be regarded as the connecting link between the fortified castle and the 'stately home' of later times. The unit or parcel of land known as the manor (a division of England dating back to the Norman conquest), when it was not the property of the Crown or the Church, belonged to a private landowner. He might be a landowner on a large scale, in which case a number of manors would be in his possession, but as circumstances changed he would dispose of certain of his acres to smaller men, thus gradually creating the class we know as the landed gentry and producing that very English character the squire. The squire might or might not be Lord of the Manor as well as owning the acres, but he had to live

Lacock Abbey, Wiltshire.

somewhere, and that somewhere was usually known as the manor-house. Possibly it may have stood on the site of a ruder dwelling provided by the original owner for his bailiff or manager; in any case, for manifest reasons it would be attached to the village; convenience, safety, and the inadequacy of communications all demanded such a situation. The village, the church and the manor-house; the people, the priest and the squire. It is no exaggeration to say that examples appear inexhaustible; England is not a large country, but listen to a group of English people interested in such matters, and you will soon find that each one has his particular 'discovery' of which the others may not even have heard. As one example I might take Mells in Somerset, where the shadow of the high church tower veers slowly like a pointing finger across the lawns of the manor garden. Or Sandford Orcas, in Dorset, where a steep little land leads up from the village to the church and to the archway of the manor alike. Or Sutton Courtney, in Berkshire, where from the end of the village street you can look up at the house through wrought-iron gates, even if you have not the privilege of walking in the garden where a wilderness of roses overhangs the Thames and mossy walls crumble among the statues behind the borders filled with flowers. Or Avebury in Wiltshire, that Downland village of strange associations, enclosed within an earthwork older than Stonehenge. Here, at Avebury, you might fail to observe the manor-house if you did not know that there was one to seek, unless, indeed a familiarity with the usual system taught you that the place to look for it was beside the church, and there you would find it, at the end of a long haunted avenue of elms, hidden round a corner, a low grey house standing within a garden enclosed by white walls thatched in the manner characteristic of walls in that part of the country. It is a steep small bit of thatching, like a miniature pent roof, which at Avebury takes a curiously witch-like quality, something like the gingerbread house of Hansel and Gretel. The stream of the Kennet runs along one side of the garden, waving the river-weeds against its ripples. The union between the flowing stream and the whitewashed thatched walls and the grey house, and the Downs beyond, so sober, so English, so typical in spite of the Druidic magic. It is difficult to resist being carried away on small streams like the Kennet to places one has seen and loved. It is hard to restrict oneself to a mere list; hard to give a bare mention to places such as St. Catherine's Court, in Somerset; Parham Park, in Sussex, with its heronry; Parnham Manor-house, in Dorset; Chastleton, in Oxfordshire; Cranborne and Athelhampton, in Dorset; Stanton Old Hall, in Derbyshire (where the sword of the great-great-great-grandfather of the present tenant still hangs in the kitchen); Stanway and Bibury Court and Owlpen, in Gloucestershire – ah, what a dream is there! Owlpen, that tiny grey manor-house, cowering

Leeds Castle, Kent.

amongst its enormous yews, yews that make rooms in the garden with walls taller than any rooms in the house; dark, secret rooms of yew hiding in the slope of the valley.

They vary in size, these houses, but as a rough generalisation it may be said that they are convenient and manageable. A second category, less properly to be reckoned among the manors, fortunately for their owners in these days, do not quite equal the enormous piles which we shall see arising towards the end of the sixteenth century. The houses in this second category are large, but not overwhelming, and, again restricting myself to the tantalising system of giving a mere list, I stand bewildered before the wealth I have to choose from: shall I include Barrington Court, in Somerset; Mapperton, in Dorset; Levens Hall, in Westmorland, that pale house with its topiary gardens; the Vyne, in Hampshire, of brick and stone; Ashby St. Ledgers, in Northampton; Burton Agnes, in Yorkshire; Burton Constable, also in Yorkshire; and that fine Buckinghamshire mansion, Chequers, built somewhere round 1565, and now assigned for ever by the generosity of Lord Lee of Fareham as the country residence of the Prime Ministers of England?

Chequers is a country house which any squire might love. What then shall we say of Littlecote, in Wiltshire, the home of the wild Darells? Littlecote is long and low and pink, with mullioned windows and forty gables of simple proportions; the garden behind the house is all that an English garden should be; lawns as perfect as those of an Oxford college, flower borders designed with a perfect regard for a most unusual combination of colours, a water-garden fed by that same Kennet which flows past Avebury.

For the continuity of history, you could scarcely have a better example of it than at Littlecote, where a Roman tessellated pavement was uncovered in the park, revealing that this sixteenth-century house stands on the site of a villa once belonging to some rich provincial Roman more than a thousand years earlier.

If I had to choose only one of the moderate-sized houses (as distinct from the little manor-house and the greater country house) to show a stranger an example of what our domestic architecture could produce during the sixteenth century, Littlecote would certainly have a strong claim. But then I should also have to consider Bramshill, which, although somewhat later in date (it was not completed externally until 1612) and built on a nobler scale than Littlecote, shares much of Littlecote's rosy beauty. It has the characteristic long gallery, the ornamental plaster-work ceilings, the tall mantelpieces of mixed marble. Lovely inside and out, Bramshill, standing among the fine trees and bracken of its park, offers as fair a picture as any house in England.

But what about Haddon in Derbyshire, standing above the Wye, which may share with Penshurst the

The Terrace, Haddon Hall, Derbyshire.

claim to be one of the most romantic of our houses? romantic both in their appearance and in the lives of those who lived in them. Love and poetry hang about them, floating like flags from the tower-tops. With Haddon and Penshurst and Hardwick we climb up the rungs of the ladder which will lead us finally to such great Elizabethan piles as Montacute and Longleat, Hatfield and Knole. Haddon took 550 years in the building, a very good example of the gradual growth which culminates in a perfect unity.

Hardwick in Derbyshire, has a different story, for it was built all of a piece in seven years, 1590 to 1597, by a commanding lady who married four husbands; bullied and survived them all; lived to the age of ninety (1518 to 1608), spent her life 'proud, furious, selfish and unfeeling, a builder, a buyer and seller of estates, a money-lender, a farmer, and a merchant of lead, coals and timber.' Not only did she build Hardwick, but also Oldcotes, Worksop, Bolsover and Chatsworth – not the present Chatsworth, but an earlier house which was begun in 1557 and pulled down in 1688. Not content with all this, she also saw to it during her lifetime that a fine monument to her memory should be put in Derby, the grand disagreeable old lady whose husbands' names are now forgotten, but who comes imperishably down to us as Bess of Hardwick.

'Four times the nuptial bed she warmed,
And every time so well performed
That when death spoiled each husband's billing
He left the widow every shilling.'

Hardwick is an unusual house.
Its speciality is its enormous windows:

'Hardwick Hall,
More glass than wall.'

But, apart from its exterior, the interior is exuberant with the fantasy of a rich imagination. The raised plaster-work of the so-called Presence Chamber, with its hunting scenes and strange forest landscape, the curiously original staircase, the wealth of tapestry, the swaggering coat-of-arms – all make one feel that there must have been something about the magnificent Bess to justify the witch's prophecy that when she ceased to build she would die. A spell of hard frost stopped her building one winter, and die she duly did.

Coming from Hardwick to Penshurst in Kent is like coming from the abode of a giant to the graceful gracious dwelling of ladies. One feels that all the inhabitants of Penshurst must have been delicate and fair. The rough old banqueting hall is almost out of place; it should not belong to the dreamy house and green-

hedged garden. Yet with its ogived Gothic windows it makes half the beauty of the garden front; the stone tracery of the windows of that hall, built in 1340, melts perfectly though differently into the Elizabethan house tacked on to the earlier building, another example of how the English house has grown little by little throughout the centuries.

Sir Philip Sidney lived here at Penshurst, and the Earl of Leicester, beloved of Queen Elizabeth, and Saccharissa, beloved of Edmund Waller, the statesman loved by a queen, the woman loved by a poet – history and poetry all mixed up. An English country centre of courtliness, gaiety and culture which we may favourably compare with the court of Urbino and Castiglione's *Cortegiano*, although the small provincial Kentish court of the Sidneys and their ladies and poets must have been far less boring and self-conscious than the Court of Urbino with its interminable conversations lasting from dusk to dawn. I imagine that the English conversation of the Sidneys and their friends at Penshurst flowed more elastic and less organised than the conversations at Urbino. English people do not like being organised; they like to live their own lives as best seems to them. The Sidneys, in fact, were living their own lives at Penshurst and talking in their own way, freely and gaily, in the same free and elastic way as Englishmen were building their houses all over the country; according as their taste and income allowed them. I fancy that any

English aristocratic intellectual house-party in 1610 would not have differed very much from the equivalent house-party held at any time between the years 1912–1939. The Cecils must have talked in very much the same way at Hatfield in 1610 as the Cecils at Hatfield might talk in 1939, with the same mixture of political and intellectual interests, switching over from one to the other; and so, I imagine, a family party of the Sidneys at Penshurst must have run over all the happenings of life, skating gracefully from one subject to the other, never dwelling ponderously on anything, but always touching delicately and briefly, in the true sense of Humanism.

From Penshurst we come to its great neighbour Knole, separated only by a few leafy miles of the Kentish Weald. One of the largest houses in England, Knole may stand as representative of the enormous homes erected for themselves by the Elizabethan and Jacobean nobility. Yet here again we find that Knole grew, and that its gables (which give it so peculiarly Elizabethan a character) were added to an earlier structure. Once the palace of the Archbishop of Canterbury, then a royal palace, Knole came to its fulfilment as the home of an English family in whose hands it has remained ever since 1586. It is an interesting example of a house which, although so vast in extent (being built round a system of seven courtyards and covering over five acres of ground), is yet perfectly subdued in its external parts. You could not isolate any separate

Knole, Kent.

section and say, 'This was built for display.' The grey and green courtyards are quiet as a college; the garden paths suited to the pacings of scholars as well as of courtiers; its 'stately and tempered medievalism' lacks all taint of the *nouveau riche*. The interior, contrariwise, is richly decorated. Elizabethan and Jacobean interiors always were. There are the long galleries, the elaborate plaster ceilings, the grand staircase with the heraldic leopards sitting on top of the newels, the sumptuous furniture of velvet and brocade, the curtained beds, the polished floors, the panelled rooms, the stained glass of the heraldic windows. I have often wondered about the everyday life of the inhabitants of houses such as Knole and Penshurst, Haddon and Hardwick, Hatfield and Longleat, Cobham and Chequers, Bramshill and Apethorpe. How did they live? They built their grand houses to suit their desire for a home, but, having built them, they must have been in a quandary how to keep themselves and their guests warm. I imagine that they must all have crowded round the fireplace in a long gallery, the gallery which was the living-room and of which we show a typical example from Hardwick on page 38. Those long galleries must have been draughty and cold unless you crouched and crowded round the big fireplace or got into the big bed and drew the curtains round you and shut yourself into the black secrecy of love and sleep with mistress or with wife. The bedroom with the huge curtained bed was usually situated at the end of the long gallery. It might, as at Knole, be the bedroom assigned to the Venetian Ambassador or to the King, or to a poet, or to an archbishop of Canterbury, or to Charles the Second spending a night there with Nell Gwyn.

This, as I see it, was the way in which the cultured Englishman of the sixteenth century built his house, conversed, shivered, hunted, entertained his friends, drank, and snored. His prodigious household dined at long tables in the banqueting hall, while he and his family, his guests and his chaplain dined at an upper table in the same room at the same time. His household occupied long galleries also, but they were at the top of the house, attics running the whole length of one wing just under the roof. At Knole, for example, these attics are still known as the Retainers' Galleries and a list dated 1623 still hangs from a nail giving the names of over a hundred 'retainers,' with their various employments.

One must not forget sport, that manifestation of masculine activity which always played so large a part in English country life, and which is so intimately associated with the English country house. Outdoor life has always been more important to the English country gentleman than the indoor; the field more alluring than the hearth. In one picture we reproduce, the owner of Melford Hall, in Suffolk, Sir Hyde Parker, is shown with his house in the background and his dogs well to the front, also his bag for the day – not a very good bag considering that he had got a neighbour over to join him in a day's shooting: two partridges and one hare. One of the dogs, in default of game, carries his master's top hat.

The picture of Sir Hyde Parker and his neighbour is interesting because it includes the portrait of his gamekeeper, whose name is also recorded: Thomas Petch. We may be apt to think of the old country squire as a snob, but this is not true. I do not believe that any caste snobbishness ever existed between the English squire and his people. A foundation of reality between them entirely levelled all class feeling. Thomas Petch, the keeper, takes his place as a matter of course beside Sir Hyde Parker, his neighbour, and his house. They are all part of the same system of life.

Melford Hall, Suffolk, 1840.

VII

THIS MAY BE A CONVENIENT PLACE TO MENTION TWO specialised and localised types of building which cannot be omitted from a general survey. I refer first to the style we call black-and-white, and then to the brickwork of East Anglia. Black-and-white describes itself; it means those timbered houses constructed of heavy beams set into pale plaster. Startling and stripy in their effect, a few famous houses of this type are concentrated in Cheshire. Chester itself is renowned for its streets of black-and-white houses, and very crooked they are too, owing to the yielding subsoil of salt. Moreton Old Hall (1559) and Gawsworth (also of the sixteenth century), two of the best known examples, are both in Cheshire; Speke Hall, that haunt of owls (1490 with later additions), is only just over the Lancashire border. Hall i' the Wood, with its attractive name (1583 with later additions) is in Lancashire likewise. But, although these are the more celebrated timber houses, it must not be thought that this convenient and very native style was limited to those two north-western counties. Humbler examples are to be found all over the country, in the yeoman's house, the farmhouse, and the labourer's cottage; in the village streets also, their tigerish gables overhanging the little shop windows below. It would be difficult to single any out of the many thousand for special mention. Stoneacre at Otham in Kent, Paycocks at Coggleshall in Essex (*circa* 1500, an interesting mixture of brick and beams), but the number is legion. They have their charm, especially when the plaster work is decorated, or, more correctly, 'pargetted,' by the comb of the local craftsman; it is a charm which is entirely indigenous and countrified; and to inhabit one of these roughly put together old houses is rather like living in an old ship: it creaks in a high wind, it creaks and leaks and yields, but one has the feeling of being very closely associated with the elements, as though one were on the sea or living in a tree-top, no bad analogy since these rural dwellings were as a matter of course constructed out of the oaks that could be cut down on the local soil. Much of the charm is lost when we come to the over-enriched specimens such as Gawsworth and Moreton Old Hall, where the simple craft becomes self-conscious. It was not an art that ought ever to have been over-elaborated.

Brickwork is a different question. Brick is in itself a more sophisticated form of building, a matter for the architect to deal with rather than for the carpenter and the plasterer. Much beautiful brickwork is to be found in England, but in this paragraph I want especially to mention a certain definite type of gatehouse which happened in East Anglia. Strange tall towers got put up; they were almost skyscrapers some of them. Layer Marney (1500–1523) rose to eight storeys in the cold east Essex air; Oxburgh Hall, in Norfolk (1482); Gifford's Hall, in Suffolk (early sixteenth century); the Deanery at Hadleigh, in Suffolk (fifteenth century); Gedding Hall, in Suffolk (sixteenth century); Melford Hall, in Suffolk. Parham Old Hall, in Suffolk, has no tall gatehouse, but is beautifully built of brick reflected into its moat.

These are the outstanding houses and gatehouses in East Anglia, but it must not be thought that similar gatehouses of brick did not occur elsewhere. We have already mentioned Hurstmonceux Castle, in Sussex. We might add Bolebrook, in Sussex, and Sissinghurst Castle, in Kent.

Parham Old Hall, Suffolk.

VIII

SO FAR I HAVE SAID LITTLE ABOUT THE INTERIORS OF these English houses. I now seem to have arrived at the point which I might usefully say something. I think the characteristic is that the inside has 'grown' in the same way as the outside has grown. There is no question of a 'period' room, so beloved of professional decorators. Everything is muddled up. You may find Jacobean panelling, Chippendale tables, Chinoiserie wallpapers, Carolean love seats, Genoa velvets, Georgian brocades, Burgundian tapestries, Queen Anne embroideries, William-and-Mary tallboys, Elizabethan bread cupboards, and even Victorian sideboards, all in such a mixture as to make the purist shudder. There was no such thing as a purist period-room decoration. Every owner acquired furniture, pictures, tapestries, statuary, *au fur et à mesure*, as the taste and fashion of his age suggested. Sometimes the taste of his age was 'good', sometimes 'bad'; there is no Absolute in such matters. Our appreciation depends on the taste and fashion of our own immediate age. We may esteem one style and condemn another. The next generation may reverse all our ideas. Where is the Dictator of Taste to say who is right and who wrong, what is 'good' and what is 'bad'? All we know is that our ancestors piled up their possessions generation by generation, and somehow managed to create a whole which is far more of a whole than any whole deliberately composed. It must be admitted that the inclination of the Elizabethan and Jacobean craftsmen was to over-do their imagination. The excitement of that adventurous age tended to express itself too exuberantly. The *débordement* of the Italian Renaissance expressed itself in England not only by an overflowing but by an overloading. The English, taking a great deal from Italy, ran away with it. They went wild, they went headstrong. The southern wind of Italian inspiration proved too much for their northern heads. Let us face it: Elizabethan and Jacobean taste could be atrocious, and frequently was. It was never safe, tidy and quiet as the taste of the succeeding century.

Amongst other manifestations of this late sixteenth and early seventeenth-century decoration the characteristic plaster work must not be forgotten. The frieze at Hardwick has already been mentioned, and, although it may stand as perhaps the most elaborate example of the art during those years, it must be realised that no great house of the period was without its embossed and pendentive ceilings, its overmantels, its panels, producing an effect of richness like the outpouring of a cornucopia. The palace of Nonesuch, begun in about 1538 for Henry VIII, provided the first example of this Italian craft. I have no space here to go into the development of the plasterer's work in England, but must content myself by saying that by the middle of the century an enterprising Englishman who had travelled in France and Italy, Charles Williams by name, was taking the monopoly away from the foreign artisans and was offering his services not only to the builder of Longleat but also to Bess of Hardwick herself. This Charles Williams was really the founder of the English school of stuccoists. The fashion caught on; Hardwick, Haddon, Burton Agnes, Knole, Plas Mawr in Wales, Audley End, Canons Ashby, Broughton, Hatfield, Longleat, Emral Hall, Chastleton Manor, Blickling, Bramshill, Langleys, all became bumpy and bossy. Leaves sprouted; sprays were flung; monograms were interlaced; mermaids, sea-horses, and grape vines twirled their tails and tendrils round the Long Gallery at Burton Constable; heraldic animals squatted guardant or lifted a paw rampant; more homely animals, such as the rabbit and the deer, came to life quaintly; Adam delved beneath his tree; giants wrestled; pomegranates were spilled; arabesques wandered. Ceilings, panels, friezes, all became crowded with a muddle of imagination, poetry, and realism in very much the same way as English literature became crowded with Italian ideas at the same time.

Burton Constable, Yorkshire, 1879.

It is, I think, worthy of comment that the Tudor age in England should have taken as extravagantly to Italian stucco-work as in literature it took to Italian comedy and tragedy, yet giving a native twist to both.

IX

ROUGHLY SPEAKING, IT MAY BE SAID THAT OUR domestic architecture during the seventeenth century became more sophisticated and less pictur-esque. It was getting itself tidied up. It became neater and more symmetrical. It straggled less. It became more deliberate and intentional, and less haphazard. We calmed down. We lost something; we gained something. We lost the rich extravagance of youth; we gained the sobriety of early middle age. We ceased to be twenty and passed into being thirty years old. Architecturally speaking, we ceased to be very young, but were not yet quite grown up.

The difference and change which took place during the first half of the seventeenth century were largely due to the rise of the architects. In July, 1573, a son was born to a clothmaker named Jones. Not an unusual name. The unusual things about this particular young Jones were his genius, which was considerable, and his baptis-mal name, which was Inigo. He may fairly be called our

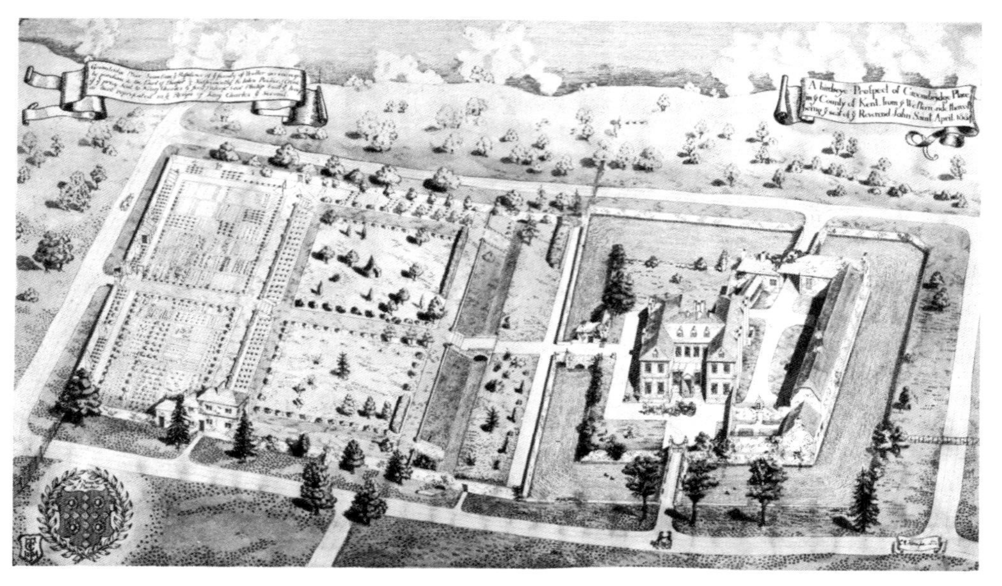

Groombridge Place, Kent, during the reign of Charles II.

first professional architect. Before his day the architect (if there was one) had remained anonymous; the builder had been all-important, probably a local man with a good practical knowledge of his job but very little generalised theory of what he was doing, who just built according to his native tradition, rather like a bird building its nest. This *naïveté* had its charm, and in many instances, as we have seen, the result was pleasing, but Inigo Jones altered all that. He got Lord Pembroke to send him to Italy, and while he was there he made the best use of his time. He discovered amongst other things that the Italians built their palaces and villas according to plan. He discovered, above all, the existence of Palladio.

He came back to England full of these novel ideas. The designer of houses in Italy was an architect, therefore the designer of houses in England should be an architect also; it should be Inigo Jones.

Many country houses claim him, and it would need a whole chapter to argue their separate claims. Some are disputed, others not. Cobham in Kent, claims him; the pavilion at Stoke Bruerne, Castle Ashby, Stoke Park and Kirby Hall, all in Northamptonshire; Forde Abbey, Brympton d'Evercy and Hinton St. George, all in Somerset; and Raynham, in Norfolk.

In point of fact it is now thought probable that the Banqueting House in Whitehall and the Queen's House at Greenwich must be regarded as the only two buildings which may without question be ascribed to Jones. The fact remains that Jones by his designs and studies exercised the strongest influence over an entire school of followers, such as John Webb, Pratt, Hugh May, Captain Wynne (a Dutchman), and that remarkable adventurer Sir Balthaser Gerbier.

I hope I do not exaggerate the importance of Inigo Jones. He may not have been so great an architect as his master Palladio, nor so great an architect as his successor, Sir Christopher Wren, but at any rate he was responsible for this quietly revolutionary change to which I have alluded, the change which brought the architect into the forefront and pushed the builder back into his proper place. My admiration for him increases when I remember that he put a little note at the end of his copy of Palladio's *Architecture*, a prescription which, he says, cured him of the sharp vomitings he had suffered from for thirty-six years. A man who can suffer from dyspepsia like that and who yet can alter the whole character of English architecture does deserve one's respect.

To the above remarks I must add a qualification. I am aware that it is not entirely correct to claim for Inigo Jones the honour of being our first named and professional architect. I shall be told that I have forgotten John Shute, who as early as 1550 was sent to Italy by the Duke of Northumberland to study architecture; or Robert Lyminge, the designer or part designer of

Hatfield, who had a hand also in the construction of Blickling; John Thorpe, who was working between 1570 and 1610, and who is associated with Montacute, Burghley House, Longford Castle, and Kirby Hall; and even Robert Smithson, who worked under John of Padua at Longleat, and who may have been responsible for that most deplorable example, Wollaton Hall. But, as has frequently been pointed out, these men were less to be regarded as architects than as surveyors of the work in progress, appointed by the builder-contractor. The truth seems to be that the functions of designer and surveyor were not sharply divided until the advent of Inigo Jones with his definite theories and foreign experience, and that there is therefore no need to nibble anything away from the reputation he has rightly earned.

X

IT IS NOT DIFFICULT TO DEFINE THE OUTSTANDING differences between the so-called Tudor house and the progeny begotten directly or indirectly by Inigo Jones. The difference is startling because Jones, instead of allowing the slow growth to take its usual way in England, abruptly imposed the real innovations he had brought back from Italy. The idiom of one country always startles when it first appears in another. The big sash windows, regularly spaced, the columns and pilasters, porticos and pediments, the straight lines, the symmetry and unity of such houses as Tyttenhanger, in Hertfordshire (1654), Ramsbury, in Wiltshire (about 1680), or Squerries Court, in Kent (1680), demonstrate the difference between the sixteenth century and the seventeenth. The wildly adolescent experiments fade out; they are replaced by deliberately planned constructions, satisfying to the eye, convenient to live in, *classic* rather than *romantic*, to use two accepted though ill-defined words. Actually, no one knows who introduced the sash-window into England, or at what date. The first mention of them occurs in accounts for work at Windsor Castle between 1686–88. This is all the more curious, as few features did more to alter the character of external architecture or the façade of the house.

Once again, having turned over this fresh page of English domestic architecture, it is still important to remember that the period was one of transition and that an outstanding trait of the English character is a love of compromise. Violent changes have never been part of our make-up. It was much more in our nature either to preserve certain features to which we had long been accustomed and to adapt and modify them gradually, or else to tack the new ideas on to the existing building and hope for the best. Examples of the former method may be seen at Swakeleys in Middlesex and at Broome Park in Kent, two houses which may well be compared since they are contemporary, *i.e.* about 1638. The Tudor influence is still to be observed in the exterior gables and also in the H-shaped plan of both. The English were loth to give up their gables and recesses for the flatter perspectives dear to the importers of the Palladian style. Equally reluctant were they wholly to scrap their buildings in the native idiom in favour of the new-fangled ideas from Italy and France; rather, they would add as they had always added, and thus you get places such as Brympton where the so-called Inigo Jones garden-front is just round-the-corner from the Tudor entrance-front. These are only instances which could be multiplied.

I might mention also an example of the new, neat house built on the older site in conjunction with older but separate buildings. For this I should choose Groombridge Place, which stands with one foot in Kent and the other in Sussex, one foot in the sixteenth, the other in the late seventeenth century. Here it is possible to say that the moat and out-buildings are purely 'romantic,' the house itself purely 'classic,' with its Doric columns and the symmetry of its wings and centre. In this combination it manages to retain something of the old manor house charm, with the comfortable convenience of the well-proportioned theories introduced by Inigo Jones, continued by John Webb, and extended by Sir Christopher Wren.

The name of Wren (1632–1723) is traditionally associated with the building of Groombridge Place, but it so happens that a curious analogy exists between him and Inigo Jones: although they both exercised the deepest influence over the design of our country houses, neither Jones nor Wren was employed in building them. As we have seen, no country house can with any certainty be ascribed to Jones, and when we come to consider the career of Wren as an architect we find that his work was entirely urban. It is doubtful even if he may be credited with Belton, in Lincolnshire, or if he designed the wings at Easton Neston, in Northamptonshire (wings which in

Easton Neston, Northamptonshire, 1876.

any case were subsequently pulled down), or was connected with Chatsworth itself. True, many drawings and elevations for houses from his pencil exist, but these remain in the realm of imagined things and never found their expression in brick or stone.

On the other hand, a whole posse of architects crowd on the heels of the two masters, whose practical achievement in the matter of country seats was greatly in excess of theirs. The profession of an architect is in one respect a curious and rather sad one: so far as public fame goes, it is almost invariably anonymous. It seems unfair, and for this reason let us attach the names of these neglected men to the names of the great houses they raised. As we approach the end of the seventeenth century and the beginning of the eighteenth, the structures which we encounter do indeed deserve to be called great, in magnitude if not always in beauty. I have already mentioned John Webb, that underestimated colleague and son-in-law of Inigo Jones, who build Ramsbury in Wiltshire, Thorpe in Northamptonshire, may have altered Petworth House and the Vyne, and worked in collaboration with Jones in what is probably the noblest room in the country, the famous Double Cube at Wilton. Webb, however, should not be classed with those overloaders of the English earth to whom we shall come in a moment; nor, perhaps, should Nicholas Hawksmoor, whose major work at Easton Neston, in Northamptonshire, shows a restrained, dignified exterior

Lumley Castle, County Durham.

entirely in the new fashion, with flat roofs, spacious windows, square angles, flattened pilasters. Hawksmoor deserves all the more credit for this sobriety, for he belongs to a generation later than Webb (his Easton Neston, for instance, was built between 1702 and 1713, whereas Webb's Thorpe Hall was about fifty years earlier), and Webb himself was eventually more influenced by Vanbrugh than by Wren, whose assistant he had been. Even so late as 1722 it was possible for men to be building 'big' houses, and yet keeping them within reasonable bounds; witness Colin Campbell, who put up Houghton, in Norfolk, for Sir Robert Walpole at that date. Campbell was also responsible for Mereworth, in Kent (1720). Mereworth deserves mention in these pages not because it is a typical English house but because it is so very much the reverse, a freak, a unique instance of a house built entirely on the Italian model, a replica in fact of Palladio's famous Villa Capra, near Vicenza. The only other house in England which might be compared with Mereworth was a villa at Chiswick designed by Robert Boyle, Earl of Burlington (1695–1753) for his own occupation. This Lord Burlington is an interesting character. An aristocrat by birth, living in an age when it was fashionable for the nobility to patronise the arts, he seems to have cared for architecture for its own sake, not merely as the pastime of a rich man. The drawings of Palladio were published at his expense and so were the drawings left by John

Webb, entitled *Designs by Inigo Jones*. Apart from these various publications, which had an extensive influence on the taste of the day, Lord Burlington, with his wealth and amateur enthusiasm, was able to set up as the patron of a group of professional architects, of whom the most renowned were William Kent and Giacomo Leoni, the respective designers of Holkham and Moor Park. So great was Lord Burlington's belief in the ability of William Kent, who he had 'discovered' in Rome, that not only did he house him at Burlington House during his lifetime, but buried him in his family vault after his death. It was perhaps a pity that Lord Burlington should not have contented himself with his publications and his benefactions, but must needs practise the art himself, for his value as a patron was greater than his value as an architect. Lord Chesterfield made a disobliging comment on a house which Lord Burlington had designed for the famous military roadmaker General Wade: he said that if the General's house was impossible to live in for his comfort, he would be well advised to take a house opposite and look at it.

This may have been a fair comment on the house Lord Burlington wanted to build for General Wade, but I cannot feel it is a fair comment on the middling houses of that period, the period which includes such houses as Ditchley, in Oxfordshire, built by James Gibbs in 1722; or Reigate Priory, in Surrey, or Ven House, in Somerset (*circa* 1700), Honington Hall, in Warwickshire (*circa*

1680), Reddish Manor, in Wiltshire, Widcombe Manor House, near Bath, two anonymous houses contemporaneous (1736) with the Woods, father and son, the architects of Prior Park, near Bath, and of many finely designed streets and squares in Bath itself. To this period also belonged Stoke Edith, in Herefordshire, destroyed by fire some years ago. This was built between 1697 and 1699 to the order of Thomas Foley, the son of a nail manufacturer. Foley became Speaker of the House of Commons, and the house remained in the possession of his family. The five successive wives of a later Thomas Foley embroidered the wall hanging showing the design of a formal garden (*circa* 1740) worked by these patient ladies. The house in the background is probably intended as a representation of Stoke Edith itself. One wonders how much and in what spirit each of them speculated on her predecessor as she stitched?

The middling houses of England during this period, say, 1670 to 1780, may be counted among the most quietly charming, convenient, and decent houses ever built. Decent, I think, is the adjective they best deserve. They are unassuming. They are as quiet as the country squire and the country existence where they belonged. They take their place, in the seventeenth and eighteenth centuries, as opposite numbers to the Gothic or early Tudor or Elizabethan or Jacobean muddles which preceded them. They belong to an England which, architecturally, was beginning to grow up.

Many things might be said about these middling houses, but the chief thing to be said is that they accommodate themselves well into the English landscape. This characteristic of the English country house was one of the first things I tried to emphasise at the beginning of this monograph, and now, as I arrive into the late seventeenth and early eighteenth centuries, I must emphasise once more the peculiar genius of the minor English house for fitting into its surroundings. The castle, the pseudo-castle, the Tudor house, the Jacobean house, they all fitted in. The only time when they went wrong was whenever they outgrew their native idiom and swelled beyond the small vernacular adapted to their small island. England is not an exciting country, considered in terms of landscape. We have no dramatic mountain ranges, no grand valleys, no enormous splits in our earth compared with the canyons of Arizona. We have no extravagant climatic or geological accidents such as typhoons, hurricanes or earthquakes. We have no extremes of climate; we are never much too cold or much too hot. This moderation reflects itself in our temperament. We are not excessive in any direction, and this lack of exaggeration which is both the strength and the weakness of our racial make-up, this sense of proportion, this Englishness which exasperates those born with a more excitable, more Latin nature, finds its expression in our national architecture.

The moderation of the English temperament thus found something satisfactory to itself in the neat and tidy houses born of the new fashion. It may seem curious that the grandeur of the Italian model should ever have accommodated itself to the exigencies of the English Cathedral Close, the English small country town, the English village street, the English parkland and the squire's estate. Yet so it was. We took the style and broke it down to our own needs. Once again we took something from Italy. As in literature our Elizabethan poets took extravagant Italian romances and piled-up murders and then turned them into dramas of the English stage, so, later, in terms of architecture, did we take and adapt the Italian classical tradition to our own mild requirements. We tempered it, and on this principle I think one may safely say that the smaller houses of the seventeenth and eighteenth centuries adapted themselves to requirements of decency and convenience quite as well as the sixteenth century English house adapted itself to the more romantic requirements of its own day. To pass through England with such considerations always present in the mind, trying them out on every example encountered, is to double the interest and amusement and speculation which such a journey provokes. It is not enough mildly to enjoy the pleasant frontages we espy over the hedge or as our motor car travels along the streets of villages and little towns. Pleasant indeed they are, with their porticos and pediments, bay-windows and sash-windows, and all they offer of agreeable rooms within: rooms largely and calmly panelled in ivory-painted wood, with alcoves for china-shelves scooped into the walls, elegant Chinese Chippendale chairs and writing-tables nicely disposed, chintzes on the arm-chairs and sofas; in short, not the homes of the grand nobility nor of the *nouveaux riches* of that day, but the homes of the country gentry or the middle-class, the quiet, solid English upper middle-class, the doctors and the solicitors and the archdeacons, *hommes de robe* rather than *hommes d'épée. Hommes de robe de chambre.* Tame, it may be said. True; but the English are always tame until they become fierce. They prefer being tame to fierce.

The interest of driving through England is enhanced if we drive in this noticing spirit. It is amusing to guess at the date of the little house we pass and then to verify our guess by the guide-book or subsequent enquiry. It is salutary to discover how far out we may be in our reckoning. The earlier centuries may well bewilder us with their congeries and conglomerations, but in this later period we must take shame if, nine times out of ten, the deliberate design does not proclaim its reign.

XI

BUT THESE GENERALISATIONS MUST SUFFICE, AND FROM the agreeable small middling house we must pass on to the monsters of construction which provoked the poet to exclaim:

> ' "Thanks, sir," I cried, " 'tis very fine,
> But where d'ye sleep or where d'ye dine?
> I find by all you have been telling,
> That 'tis a house, but not a dwelling." '

The name of Vanbrugh (1663–1726) has already once been mentioned, and its enormous shadow darkens the pages. Colossal, charmless, graceless, his achievement cannot be denied the quality of magnificence, but the present writer may not be alone in regretting that its scope could not be limited to the erection of public buildings in our cities instead of loading our counties with incongruous palaces. Supposing the employment of Vanbrugh and Inigo Jones could be reversed. No one could wish to forego Jones' work at Whitehall, but the thought of the country houses that Jones might also have built is too tantalising to be considered. Conversely, what county halls, what government offices, what theatres and opera houses, what pump rooms, what colleges, might all have come from Vanbrugh's sketch-book! It is almost (not quite) as tantalising as the vision of a London laid out by Wren.

Instead of the municipal work with which Vanbrugh might so well have been charged, we have to thank the private patron for most examples of his alarming genius. The Duke of Ancaster at Grimsthorpe, in Lincolnshire; the Earl of Manchester at Kimbolton, in Huntingdon; Sir Edward Southwell at King's Weston, in Gloucestershire; the painter, Sir Godfrey Kneller, at Whitton Hall, near Hounslow; the Earl of Suffolk at Audley End, in Essex; Lord Cobham at Stowe, in Buckinghamshire; and, above all, the Earl of Carlisle at Castle Howard, in Yorkshire (partially destroyed by fire in November, 1940), were among those who secured the services of this architect, who was not really a trained architect at all but a dramatist by profession. I cannot here relate the extraordinary career of Vanbrugh, and must only observe that it would be surprising were Mr. Noel Coward suddenly to take to architecture and begin erecting some of the most ambitious piles of masonry ever put together in this country. It was Lord Carlisle who was first responsible for setting Vanbrugh off on this second half of his career; Lord Carlisle who, round about the year

Seaton Delaval, Northumberland.

1700, entrusted him with the construction of Castle Howard, in Yorkshire, to replace the old castle of Hinderskelf on a neighbouring site. It seems likely that Castle Howard was intended as a rival to the enormous palace of Chatsworth in Derbyshire, which William Talman was engaged in raising for the Duke of Devonshire. It is comforting to reflect that Castle Howard was never quite so large as Vanbrugh intended it to be. Its tremendous façade, rounded off by cupolas, is surely enough to satisfy the most liberal taste, but Vanbrugh had dreamt of something more. He got his chance at Blenheim, where the resources of the British Treasury were (as he believed) at his disposal in the gift the nation wished to offer the victorious Duke of Marlborough.

'England's biggest house for England's biggest man.'

Perhaps as this essay is supposed to be concerned only with houses that are still inhabited I ought not to mention Seaton Delaval in Northumberland, which to my mind is the jewel of Vanbrugh's work. Partially burnt in 1822 when the jackdaws' nests in a chimney caught fire, derelict now, cracked by underground tunnelling, and blackened by the grime of the coal country, Seaton Delaval, with its fat columns and finely proportioned side-wings, has all the grand manner in miniature. It is a sad place; the grass grows rough where it should be a sward, and in the central hall where nothing echoes but one's own footsteps, the leprous plaster hangs loosely above the niches and the broken statues of Music, Painting, Geography, Sculpture, Architecture and Astronomy. Inevitably one sees in Seaton Delaval the prophecy of a fate which may await many other houses, not indeed due to the geographical accident of coal-mining, but to the deeper cause of social and economic adjustment.

XII

I HAVE ALLUDED, PERHAPS TOO VIOLENTLY, TO THE LACK of grace and charm in the works of Vanbrugh. Vanbrugh never catered for such qualities as grace and charm; he supplied only the demand for magnificence exacted by his own day. If ever there was a clumsy genius with flashes of a lighter inspiration, that was Vanbrugh. No such charge of clumsiness can be brought against the brothers Adam, who succeed him chronologically in the list of English architects. The brothers Adam were elegant and delicate in the extreme. The most surprising thing about them is that they were brothers, not sisters. There were four of them, Robert, James, John, and William. Robert (1728-1792) and his brother James, who was associated with him in all his works, are the two that count. They delighted in the lighter classical mould: niches, lunettes, bas-reliefs, chimney-pieces, and furniture designed to match the outside building. Elegant both inside and out, the Adam brothers imposed quite as strongly as Inigo Jones a new style on the English house. It is idle to speak here of Osterley, near Brentford, or of Kenwood, near Hampstead, since neither of these places can now be called country houses in the right sense of the term, but fortunately the work of the Scottish brothers flowed also over the provinces. There is Kedleston, in Derbyshire (one of the many houses of the late Lord Curzon), where Robert Adam succeeded James Paine; Nostell Priory, in Yorkshire, and Compton Verney, in Warwickshire. The Grecian gracefulness flowered in rooms finely proportioned but delicately coloured as the egg of a bird. Primrose and Wedgwood blue, lemon-yellow and cream, pale green and white, it seems strange that this highly original and sophisticated style should have been the product of Scotland and Diocletian's palace at Spalato.

Not all the architects working contemporaneously with the Adam brothers observed the same restraint. The gigantic ambitions of Vanbrugh and his patrons were only too faithfully carried on in the eighteenth century by Flitcroft, Leoni, and Kent. We have already mentioned Kent and Leoni as protégés of the munificent Lord Burlington. Henry Flitcroft must be recorded as the author of that tremendous load Wentworth Woodhouse (1740), in Yorkshire, and Woburn Abbey, in Bedfordshire. Of such houses I cannot do better than quote the words of a modern architect, words which were, in fact, applied to Vanbrugh himself, but which are just as applicable here: 'How different is this effect from that of even the largest of the Elizabethan palaces! There, grandeur itself was homely. The difference cannot be attributed to increase in size; the absence of homeliness springs not even from the inevitable difference between a palace and a manor-house. It is inherent in the changed views prevalent both as to life and as to architecture.'

These words, I think, sum up the change which we have watched taking place between the sixteenth century and the eighteenth. Just as men grew heavier and more self-indulgent, so did their homes extend themselves into a pomposity different from the dashing Elizabethan spirit which built as it chose, and added and straggled and thought more of comfort than of impressiveness. The poetry of the sixteenth century was gone, and in the place of its gables and finials, its fantasy and its mistakes, its gaiety and its extravagance, stood the solid Hanoverian England of the Georges.

XIII

THIS ESSAY DRAWS TO AN END, FOR IT IS SURELY NOT necessary to give more than a passing mention to the freak architecture of the Gothic Revival. This remarkable style, however successful in Sir Charles Barry's Houses of Parliament (1840), proved ludicrously unsuited to the English counties. Many attempts have been made to explain this return to the spikes and battlements of another age; it has been blamed on Sir Walter Scott whose own home, Abbotsford, supplies a perfect example, and on Lord Byron whose family place, Newstead Abbey, happened to reflect the popular conception of his wild career. The romances of the one, the poems and personality of the other ... It is not to be denied that the arts, as usual, were striding hand in hand; but instead of attributing too much influence to literature over architecture, it is as well to remember that both were equally susceptible to the indefinable breath of the spirit of the age. It would indeed be possible to make out a case for architecture

Inigo Jones (1573-1652)
– an engraving after the portrait by Van Dyck.

Castle Howard, Yorkshire

being first in the field. For Nicholas Hawksmoor as early as 1735 had raised Gothic towers at Westminster Abbey; in 1747 Horace Walpole had taken a lease of his famous villa at Strawberry Hill, and other seemingly paradoxical instances might be cited. It seems more reasonable, after paying due tribute to the Zeitgeist, to remark that men were becoming bored by the staid houses which had succeeded the introduction of the classic tradition. They were safe, but they were dull. And so very soon it happened that James Wyatt (1746–1813) was building Fonthill Abbey for Beckford, the author of *Vathek*, probably the most surprising construction that ever startled an English county; with his nephew Jeffry he was building Ashridge, in Hertfordshire. Charles Barry was experimenting at Toddington Manor, in Gloucestershire, with the dentated pinnacles that reappeared ten years later on his Palace of Westminster. The Pugins, father and son, by their publications greatly encouraged public taste in the Gothic direction, and at Alton Towers, in Staffordshire, the younger Pugin completed for the Earl of Shrewsbury a dwelling which might more fitly have been placed as a gate-house in the walls of Nuremberg.

This desire to escape from the respectable and rather box-like fashion found its expression not only in mediaeval turrets, baronial halls, ecclesiastical-looking windows, battlements, machicolations and spires, but also in a variety of other styles which make the beholder rub

his eyes and wonder if England once went mad. Nothing came amiss by way of a change. At least one house, Grange Park, in Hampshire, was put up as an almost exact reproduction of a Greek temple; Roman, Egyptian, and Indo-Moorish could also be supplied. Fortunately, none of these fancies enjoyed a very prolonged or extensive vogue, though few of us would welcome the disappearance of that unique oddity, the Pavilion at Brighton, completed in 1820 for the Prince Regent by John Nash. But enough of this subject, and we may rejoice that the whimsical air of novelty was so soon blown away. Had the same fate attended the later purely Gothic craze, we should be spared much to-day: St. Pancras Station, the Albert Memorial, and streets of gabled villas with stained glass in the doors.

Much has been left unsaid. Many noble houses have perforce been omitted, nor have I said a word about the gardens, which to most peoples' minds are inseparable from the picture of the English home.

The foregoing notes postulate that both the author and the reader care deeply for the things which have been herein described, in the same sense as lovers of music, painting, literature care for those things and all that they imply. But at the close of a survey of this kind, however incomplete, however telescoped, one must ask oneself what the future holds; ask it with sorrow, for the future is indeed unpromising. Even before the war the prospect was dark enough, but with war taxation and the present rate of death duties it seems improbable that any family fortune will long suffice to retain such homes in private ownership. Fortunate are those who inherit houses of manageable size, but what of those who carry the beloved burden of unreasonably spacious halls? A large house does not necessarily mean a large income, although many people seem to be under that delusion. The obligations, the responsibilities, and the expense, however, are always large.

If these English houses of ours were all to be turned into institutional buildings, schools, asylums, hotels and the like, something of our national heritage of pride and beauty would be gone. Museums? A museum is a dead thing; a house which is still the home of men and women is a living thing which has not lost its soul. The soul of a house, the atmosphere of a house, are as much part of the house as the architecture of that house or as the furnishings within it. Divorced from its life, it dies. But if it keeps its life it means that the kitchen still provides food for the inhabitants: makes jam, puts fruit into bottles, stores the honey, dries the herbs, and carries on in the same tradition as has always obtained in the country. Useful things, practical things, keeping a number of people going throughout the year. So much for the house itself, but there is the outside life too; the life in which the landlord is a good landlord, assisting his farmers, keeping his cottages in good repair, adding modern labour-saving improvements, remitting a rent in a case of hardship, employing woodmen to cut trees for his own hearth and theirs.

The system was, and is, a curious mixture of the feudal and the communal, and survives in England to-day. One wonders for how long? The only hope for these houses seems to be that they should pass into the good keeping of the National Trust.

Vita Sackville-West, 1941

SHORT BIBLIOGRAPHY

In English Homes. 'Country Life' (bound volumes). *Homes and Gardens of England*, 1932, by Harry Batsford and Charles Fry; *The English Country House*, 1935, by Ralph Dutton; *The English Castle*, 1936, by Hugh Braun; *Early Renaissance Architecture in England*, 1914, by J. Alfred Gotch; *The Manor Houses of England*, 1910, by P. H. Ditchfield (illustrated by S. R. Jones). All published by Messrs. Batsford

colour plates

Alnwick Castle, Northumberland
Arundel Castle, Norfolk
Leeds Castle, Kent
Broughton Castle, Oxfordshire
Lumley Castle, Durham
Penshurst, Kent
Inigo Jones
Castle Howard, Yorkshire

black & white illustrations

Index

Since this book was first published in 1942 many county names and boundaries have changed and some houses have been demolished. The publishers have not changed the original text. For up to date information refer to *Hudson's Historic Houses and Gardens* **available from High Wardington House, Upper Wardington, Oxfordshire, OX17 1SP.**

Acknowledgments

PRION HAVE ENDEAVOURED TO OBSERVE THE LEGAL requirements with regard to the rights of suppliers of illustrative material and would like to thank **Mary Evans Picture Library** for their generous assistance. *Parham Old Hall*, a water colour by W. C. Stanfield is reproduced courtesy of the **Victoria & Albert Museum.**